THE CHANGING

Jericho

BOOK ONE

Julie Kennedy

Robert Boyd
PUBLICATIONS

Published by
Robert Boyd Publications
260 Colwell Drive
Witney, Oxfordshire OX8 7LW

First published 1997

Copyright © Julie Kennedy and
Robert Boyd Publications

ISBN: 1 899536 14 0

OTHER TITLES IN THE
CHANGING FACES SERIES

Anyone can publish a book — why not you!

Have you ever wanted to publish a book? It is not as difficult as you might think. The publisher of this book provides a service to individuals and organisations large and small.

Advice can be given on all facets of production: typesetting, layout and design, paper stocks, styles of binding including wired, perfect, sewn, limp and cased binding, the options are almost endless. If you have a project you would like to discuss why not contact:

Robert Boyd
PRINTING & PUBLISHING SERVICES
260 Colwell Drive
Witney, Oxfordshire OX8 7LW

Printed and bound in Great Britain at The Alden Press, Oxford

Contents

Cover illustrations

Front: Empire Day at St Barnabas Infant School, 1925

Back: The North Oxford Grocery, Fruit and Plant Stores,
        Walton Street, 1958

Acknowledgements

I would like to thank all those who have helped me with this book including: the Bodleian Library; Ivor Fields (photographer); Hinkins & Frewin; R.J. Johnson & Co. Ltd; Kelly's Directory; Oxford & County Newspapers; Oxford Stamp Centre (Jeremy's); Oxford Synagogue; Oxford University Press Archives and in particular Peter Foden for his patience and help; Oxford Photographic Archives (OPA), especially Nuala la Vertue; Thomas Photographs; St Barnabas School and W. Lucy & Co. Ltd. The photographs from *The Clarendonian* on pages 10, 42, 45–47 and 93 are reproduced by kind permission of Oxford University Press, the copyright holders.

Thanks are also due to the following people who have so kindly shared their reminisences with me and lent some of the photographs included in this book: John Beesley, Thomas Blackburn, John Brucker, Steve Carr, Syd Church, Bill Clifford, Gladys Couling, Albert Eaglestone, Wendy Gray, Michael Grant, Colin Harris, Ted Harris, Betty Howes, Mr Huckin, Hugh Kearsey, David Ledger, Dennis Mason, Mrs McGuiness, Ann Mobbs, John Payne, Deanna Peedell, Mrs Perks, Mrs Prewitt, Mrs Vera Rush, Jennifer Rush, Mrs Tustin, Colin Tustin, Betty Upstone, Mrs Webster, Philip Williams, Michael Wright. I would also like to thank Christine Fenn for adapting Mr Albert Eaglestone's map; Carole Newbigging, Becky Vickers and finally my husband Pete and children Ben, Erin, Rafe and Leo for putting up with my constant absences and monopolisation of the computer!

Preface

'It soon becomes clear in conversation with those who have left the area, that Jericho remains a special place for them, and many references are made, not only to the people there, but to the church and school, or Barney's as either, or both, are often affectionately known'. Written almost a quarter of a century ago, this sentiment still holds true. Older people speak of their childhood in Jericho with such fondness that it seems idyllic despite the poverty that was commonplace. Families that moved to Jericho in the first years of its existence commonly remained for several generations and those that moved away returned for such important events as their child's christening.

Following the redevelopment of St Thomas and St, Ebbes, similar plans were in hand for Jericho. Some houses were subject to compulsory purchase orders, being declared unfit for human habitation, and sums as little as £200 paid to the occupants who may well have lived there for most of their lives. These sums were so low as they were based on the ground rent rather than the value of the property. This sad state of affairs was eventually rectified but one poor man was paid the £200 when he still owed £600 on the mortgage on the property. So began the Battle of Jericho, led by doughty local councillor Olive Gibbs. Luckily the residents of Jericho, and others in the city like Councillor Gibbs managed to halt the redevelopment; new houses were built but in keeping with the spirit of the area as well as the physical appearance.

The Oxford University Press and W. Lucy & Co. Limited have been large employers in the area for over 150 years. It is quite suprising that Jericho was originally home to several more well known employers: Johnson's, Stephenson's and Hinkins & Frewin all had premises here until comparatively recently. The amount of memorabilia from the area is quite suprising; school photographs in particular abound and it is to be regretted that more of them could not be included here. However, it is quite likely that there exists sufficient information to produce a second book on this fascinating area and consequently any photographs or information would be most welcome.

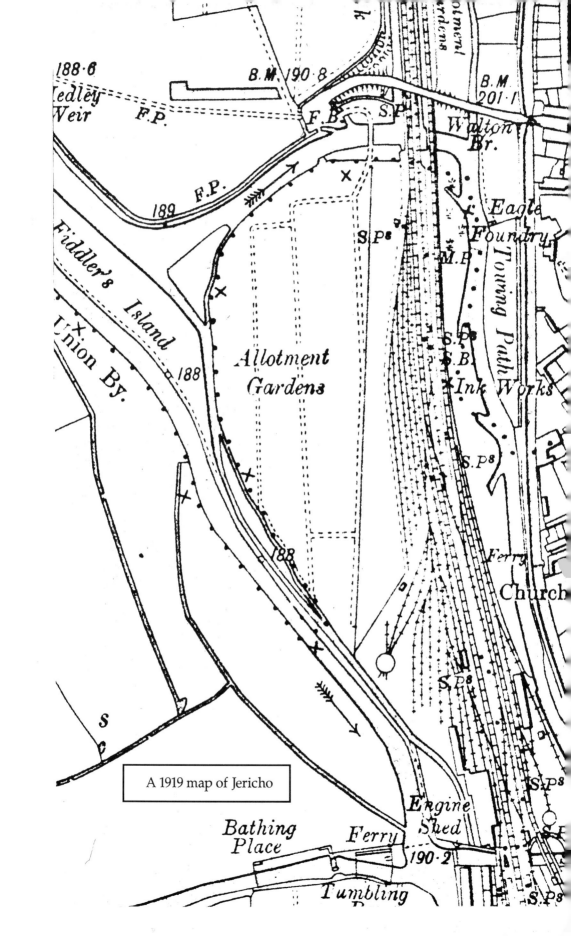

A 1919 map of Jericho

Introduction

Situated about half a mile from the old City walls, Jericho was built in the nineteenth century on land that had been largely uninhabited until then and acquired its name from Jericho Gardens which date from at least the seventeenth century and Jericho House, an inn built on this site. As late as 1860 the area to the north of Jericho House was occupied by sand pits and allotment gardens, the latter stretching to and covering Cabbage Hill, now Kingston Road. The construction of the new Oxford University Press building and the Jericho Iron and Brass Foundry (later Lucy's), coupled with the close proximity to the Oxford canal, created a need for local accommodation for those who worked in this area.

The housing, mainly brick and slate terraced, was built to suit these employees who were mainly labourers or tradesmen. Unfortunately these houses were built without even basic drainage so that epidemics of cholera were prevalent in the mid-nineteenth century. The open sewers and the flooding that was common, due to the low lying land, only aggravated the problem with too many people living too close to each other in such conditions. To the non-residents it was an area to be despised as the following scathing quotations show: In the 1860s 'not all the devoted work of the St Paul's clergy could make Jericho other than it was – a slum and a squalid slum at that'. It was also described by R.D. Blackmore in *Cripps the Carrier* '. . . a dark muddy lane leading to Jericho, down which it was not safe for a man to walk'.

Jericho's salvation was the building of St Barnabas church which, with its adherence to the Oxford Movement, played such an enormous part in the lives of every man, woman and child of the parish. By the turn of the century not only was the school centred around St Barnabas, but most other social activities took their lead from the church and its devoted clergy with the result that the parishoners became part of an extended family tied by bonds of affection to this unique area.

The social build up of the area has changed; houses today fetch high prices and university employees and students live cheek by jowl with those who have lived in the same house all their lives. The family links with the parish may not be as strong as they were and many born in Jericho have moved elsewhere in Oxford yet there is still a keen interest in Jericho by both old and new residents.

Views around Jericho

Walton Street looking towards Gloucester Green, taken in the early years of this century. Originally Walton Lane, it is probable that this was the road leading to Walton Manor and its farmlands and 'also to an old road, now destroyed, which led past Walton Well'. On the right is Worcester College; the adjacent cottages built below the level of the road date from around the 18th century. The tramlines and a tram approaching the junction with Beaumont Street are just visible. Trams remained in Walton Street until about the outbreak of World War 2; when cycling along Walton Street, one had to take great care to avoid the tramlines!

Taken in April 1908 after a snow storm, this photograph shows workmen outside the Oxford University Press clearing a pathway. The cleared track is the tramway. Horse trams were installed in Oxford in 1881 and in 1913 Oxford's first buses were operated by the Oxford Tram Co.

Walton Crescent looking down into Jericho in the early years of this century. No. 40A was the home of Harold George Grant, a builder and decorator who was born in this street as was his son Michael. Harold's father, George Arthur Grant, came to Jericho from Kirtlington  and was the manager of the Oxford Co. Partnership, Builders and Decorators. The parish boundary stone could once be found between Nos. 37 and 38. The Grants bought No. 17 Walton Crescent in 1948 for £500.

Pictured 25th June 1921 outside the Institute, the Social Club of the Oxford University Press, the annual outing (known to printers as Wayzgoose), of the jobbing department. Once the site of 'The House of Industry', on its demolition it was sold to the Rev Newman for a Roman Catholic College in 1865 but was re-sold a month later to the University when Newman's project failed to find favour with the Vatican. Seen here, front row: A. Saxton, A. Panting, P. Cox. Second row: T. Price, S. Squires, W. Gardiner jnr, J. Pimm, R. Johnson. Third row: F. Nutt, E. Fitchett, W. Hire, W. Gardiner snr. Fourth row: T. Ramsey, Harry Lapworth, H. Grundy. Fifth row: J. Lorey, Hugh Lapworth, H. Cook. Back row: W. Taylor, W. Morgan, W. Farrow. Standing: E. Boore, J. Frost, T. Griffiths. One notice from the OUP reads as follows: Wayzgoose and August Bank Holiday, 1906 'The press will be shut down from Friday August 3rd at 6.30pm till Tuesday August 7th at 8am. The Controller does not undertake to pay wages for the Holiday to any Establishment Hand who is absent from work without leave on Tuesday morning. This is the last occasion on which payment will be made for the August bank holiday'. In 1924 Mr and Mrs Goode of the Headington Poor Law Institution became Stewards of the Institute. (*The Clarendonian,* 1960s.)

Jericho House was rebuilt on or near the site of earlier building bearing the same name; this photograph was taken about 1868. Originally a small wayside inn, it was later considerably enlarged and a brewery built on the opposite side of Jericho Street which by the turn of the century was home to Hedges Exors. of corn, flour, meal and bread stores. Jericho House itself was owned for many years by the Higgins family and it is likely that it is they who are photographed outside their home. They subsequently sold the premises to Morrells brewery. Further south is the Prince of Wales public house. (By permission of the Bodleian Library: MS. Top. Oxon. d 501 fol. 174.)

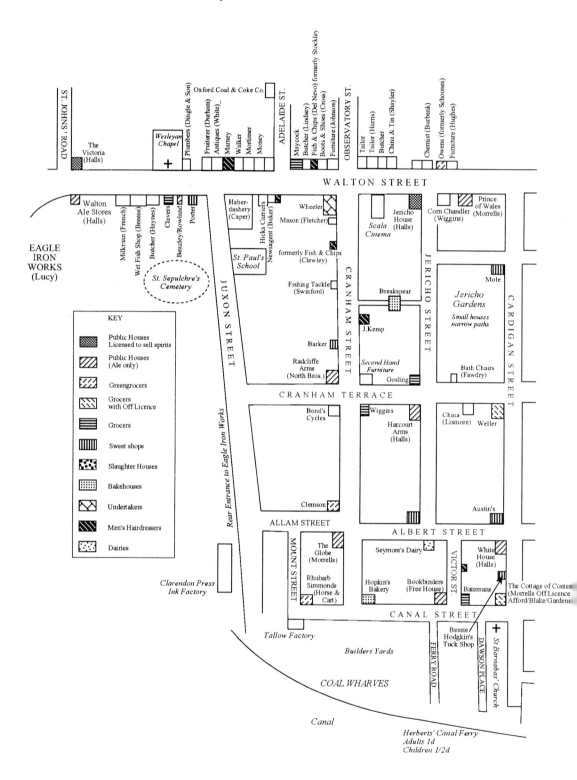

Adapted from a map of Jericho originally drawn by Albert Eaglestone based upon his reminiscences of the area.

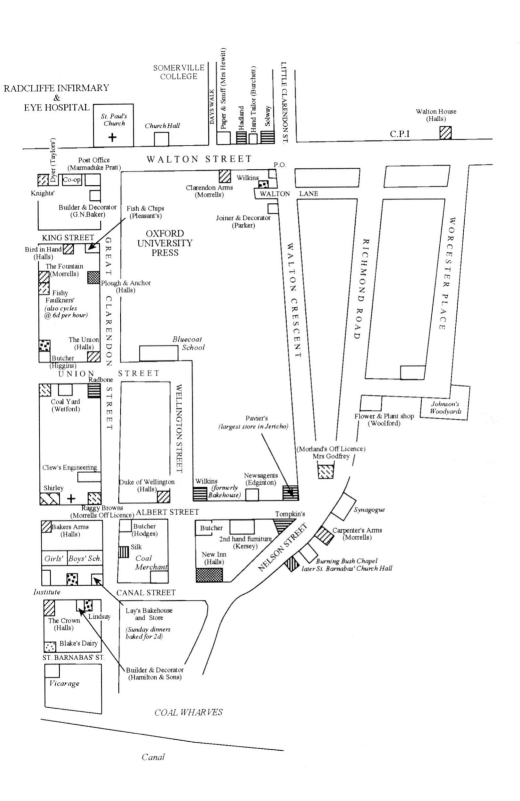

Cranham Street around 1920. The provision merchant on the right is just one of many such small businesses that could be found in almost every street in Jericho. Frequently these shops were run in the front parlour by a woman whose husband had employment elsewhere and certainly helped to make ends meet. The pub on the left is the Radcliffe Arms. These houses have since been demolished; those on the left have been replaced with modern houses and those on the right by Grantham House which provides sheltered housing.

Cardigan Street mid-1970s; the last landlord of the Fountain was Ted Murphy. Next to the Fountain Public House is Faulkner and Sons, motor cycle agents. Some of the houses have already been demolished; those at the bottom are in Union (later Hart) Street. In the nineteenth century, that part of Cardigan Street by the church was named Portland Place; this area and its surround was water-logged for most of the year and was described about 1920 by an old resident as 'being then interspersed with foul ditches, bog and marsh land'.

Looking from Union Street to the junction with Wellington Street. The building on the left of the photograph is the old Greycoat School which was used by the Oxford University Press. (Courtesy OUP Archives.)

Looking down Wellington Street towards Albert Street with many of the houses and the Greycoat School demolished. (Courtesy OUP Archives.)

An aerial view of the Oxford University Press clearly shows how it was built in the style of the Oxford Colleges, that is around a quadrangle. At the top left is the Greycoat School and running from there to the top right of the photograph is Great Clarendon Street; these houses were demolished in the 1970s. The two houses on the far right are on the corner of King Street which ran from Great Clarendon Street through to Jericho Street. The white house is the Plough and Anchor, a Hall's pub, and on the left, at the junction with Union Street, was once another pub called the Union. (Courtesy of OUP Archives.)

The back of Nos. 1 and 2 Wellington Street with the Greycoat School in the centre of the photograph. This school was founded in St Peter in the East but in 1829 this site was acquired and a school for 300 pupils plus a house for the master built. As the name suggests, the boys wore grey uniforms and after being educated they were apprenticed. The building of parish schools reduced the numbers so that in 1865 the Greycoat school was closed and the building sold to the Oxford University Press. (Courtesy OUP Archives.)

Jericho Gardens was the first clearance area in Jericho, being demolished in 1937. The houses were back to back and were probably the poorest part of Jericho with shared outside taps and outside toilets. During World War 2, air raid shelters were erected on the bottom part of Jericho Gardens although luckily they were never needed. (OPA)

Looking from Canal Street towards St Barnabas Church, once the heart of Jericho. On the left is Victor Street; Dawson Place once stood by the church where the telephone box is now situated. The houses on the right are Whitford Place.

The landlords of the Crown, Canal Street, in the 1950s were Vera and Barny Evans.

St Barnabas School in Cardigan Street being demolished. Not the entire school met this fate and some survives as housing. Inside the tower, stone steps led between floors; classrooms had pot-bellied stoves on which bowls of water were heated and at least one child was scalded when carrying this water.

Taken in the early 1960s, this aerial photograph clearly shows Johnson's builders yard and to its right the engineering workshop of F.J. Payne in Worcester Place. During World War 2, members of staff for both businesses used to take turns spending the nights fire watching in case any incendiary devices landed. Half way down on the left-hand side the only shop in Worcester Place was a little sweet

shop run by Mrs Barnes which also sold cigarettes. In the early years of the century a Dame School was run in Worcester Place by Miss King. She also ran a laundry from No. 10, a double fronted house, which ran until the mid-1940s. In the top right corner of the photograph, the left-hand terraced house at the bottom of Walton Crescent was L.G. Pavier, the largest store in Jericho.

Looking from what was King Street towards Union Street. Cardigan Street now runs only from Union Street but one can easily follow its original path through the school playground roughly parallel to the wooden fence. The school itself is built on the site of the demolished Jericho Gardens and the grass area in the foreground marks the spot where the houses between Great Clarendon Street and Cardigan Street were demolished.

Walton Well Road at the junction with Walton Street, about 1910. Lucy's Social and Sports Club is on the left; it may be that the men in the photograph have spent their lunch hour in the club and are returning to work. Kelly's Directory gives Edward Hewlett, baker and confectioner, as the occupant of the corner shop. A trackway from Walton Manor to Port Meadow lay across a ford in the Thames; at this juncture was Walton Well and in 1885 a drinking fountain was erected here by a local coal merchant, William Ward, 'to counteract the local surfeit of pubs'.

Juxon Street Wharf, unloading coal. Mrs Rose Skinner and Miss Jean Humphries. (OPA)

WALTON STREET (St. Thomas' & St.Giles'), from Worcester st. to Kingston rd.

1 Hollis Alfonso
2 Gillam Percy R
3 Ruskin College (Dennis Hird M.A. principal : C. S. Buxton B.A. vice-principal ; Bertram Wilson, gen. sec)
......here is Worcester pl......
4 National Society for the Prevention of Cruelty to Children (Oxford branch) (A. Carter, inspector) (Inspector's Office)
5 Grierson Frederick, poor rate collector for Oxford incorporation
6 Rapley Frederick G. pianoforte maker
7 Butler Edmund
8 Faulkner William Geo
9 Brimfield Mrs. lodging ho
10 Beesley Mrs
11 Chapman George Edwd. clock maker
12 Harris Charles
13 Curtis Charles Drage
14 Sawyer Mrs
.....here is Richmond rd.....
16 Alden Isaac
17 Basford-de-Wilson Rev. Fredk. Augustus M.A
19 Green Arthur, lodging ho
19 Belcher Herbt. Geo. M.A
21 Johnson Frederick Jas
22 Neale Christopher
23 Cripps Alfred
24 **COUSINS HENRY,** sign writer & grainer
25 West Thomas George, cycle agent
26. Sims Mrs. Emma, lodging house
27 Smithers Mrs
28 Tandy Miss
...... here is Walton cres......
29 Fleckner Mrs. L.M. tbcnst
29A, Barton Edward, hair dresser
30 **GIBBETT & GODFREY,** cab proprietors & jobmasters, smart, cosy carriages, broughams & victorias. Telephone No. 259
30 National Telephone Co. Ltd. (public call off)

30 Gibbett Albt. Edward, greengrocer
31 Taylor Francis Prior
32 King Mrs. servants' registry office
32 Simpson Allan
33 Horne Mrs. & Miss, school
34 Paviere Leslie. photgr
35 The Clarendon Arms P.H. Joseph Forty, propr
University Printing Office (Horace Hart M.A. (printer to the University), controller)
Oxford Magazine (published on wednesdays, during term), Horace Hart M.A. publisher (Clarendon press)
Oxford University Gazette (published during term)
Bradley Henry M.A. Ph.D. (North house)
Hart Horace M.A. (The Press house)
Miller William, lodge keeper (University press)

here is Great Clarendon st

36 Pratt Marmaduke, grocer, & post office
37 Buck Jas. lodging house
38 Thomas Miss
39 Frost Jacob
40 Bidmead George G. chimney sweep
41 & 42 Oxford Co-operative & Industrial Soc. Lim
43 Withers Wm. Ambrose, cabinet maker
43 Withers Edgar, cycle agt
44 Boyle Edmund J. professor of music
45 **Watters Charles Fredk.** coal merchant
46 Dunford George Henry
46 English Dental Co. Lim
47 Dyer Chas. R. F. tailor
48 Howes George, grocer
......here is Cardigan st ......
49 Hale Mrs
50 Baker Miss
51 Basson John
52 Crocker Frederick
53. Perry Mrs
54 Morley Frank, beer retlr
55 Wiggins J. & Sons, bakrs
...... here is Jericho st ......
56 & 57 Jericho House P.H. Harry C. Kidby

58 **SODEN WILLIAM A. & SONS,** licensed chimney sweepers & government contractors : established over a **CENTURY** at Oxford
59. Payton George Henry
60 Crapper Fdk. Thos. buildr
......here is Cranham st......
61 Wheeler Wm Hy. & Son. decorators & undertkrs
61 Wheeler William Henry, parish clerk of St. Paul's
62 Butcher Mrs
63 Walter Charles V. fencing master
64 Rolph Mrs
65 Baker W. C. picture frame ma. & news agt
66 Edwards George Hudson. tailor
67 Sumner Albert James, boot maker
68 Martin Mrs. private nursing home
68 Martin Philip Henry
69 Rivers-Willson A. Ph.D., F.C.S.E., L.S.A. Lond. physician & surgeon (surgery)
70 Gibbs Albert James, upholsterer & bedding manufacturer
71 Willis Reuben H. boot ma
72 **CAPE F. & CO.** drapers
...... here is Juxon st ......
73 Wilsdon Henry Benj
74 **Harding Charles, china & glass stores**
75 Winn Lionel Arthur
76. Herbert Chas. Hy. tailor
77 Woods Christr. Stephens
78 **ROWLAND JOHN HY.** grocer, fruiterer & greengrocer
St. Sepulchre's Cemetery (Hy. Johnson, keeper)
81 Cleaver Harry, grocer
81 Harrison Thomas
82 Timms Bros. cycle mas
82 Bayzand William Jsph
83 **BREESE JOHN,** fishmonger & poulterer
84 French George, butcher
85 Organ Edward Herbert, beer ret. & cab propr. Tel. 143

An extract from Kelly's Directory, 1908.

Employment

W. Lucy & Co. Ltd.

Traditionally dating from the late eighteenth century, the business that became W. Lucy & Co. Ltd. is first mentioned in available records in 1812. In 1825 William Carter moved his brass and iron foundry from the back of Newton Lodge, his house in Summertown, to Walton Well Road; in 1838 this foundry became known as the Eagle Ironworks. The area was undeveloped but the advantages of a business abutting the Oxford to Birmingham Canal at a time when this method of transport was predominant were obvious. William Carter's connection with the new business was brief and in 1830 he moved to Leamington leaving his partners Grafton, Baker and Briggs to continue in Jericho. In 1864 the company's name changed to Grafton & Lucy; the Lucy family lived next door to the works. By 1873 William had died of TB aged 35; the business was bought by James Kelley and was inherited by his son Charles in 1897. In the 1860s the firm's main work was the manufacture of such things as cast iron girders and pipes, ornamental ironwork, lamp-posts and a substantial amount of work for the University. Around the turn of the century a new product, cast iron shelves for libraries, was supplied in increasing numbers not only to these institutions but also to University and Government departments. The early years of the century saw the growth of the electrical side of the business with pioneer work in electrical connections resulting in orders from as far away as India. This side of the business was not always profitable and the foundry's work supported the new venture. Munitions were manufactured at Lucy's during World War 1, in particular mine sinkers and mortar bombs. After 1918 Lucy's became a well known switchgear and electrical engineering firm. During World War 2 contracts with the Armed Forces were obtained which guaranteed work for that period. The post-war era brought a successful period of modernisation and by the 1970s Lucy's had become an internationally known company, even with a branch in Saudi Arabia.

This photograph of the entrance to Lucy's at the bottom of Walton Well Road shows the proximity of the canal.

Photographed in the iron foundry in the early 1960s, on the right W. Titchener.

The iron foundry moulding machine, again in the same period.

Instruments and Current Transformer Assembly. The ladies at the right-hand end of each row have been identified as, working backwards: J. Ball, B. Baker and J. Holloway. The men in this section are J. Hanson and M. Howes (in the white coat). Towards the window in the front row wearing the white shirt is M. Howes; the gentleman further back right by the window is H. Stone.

The light machine shop staffed entirely by disabled operators, holders of 'green cards'. Photographed here in the early 1960s, at the front C. Breakspear and left to right by the window G. Bidmead and R. Veary.

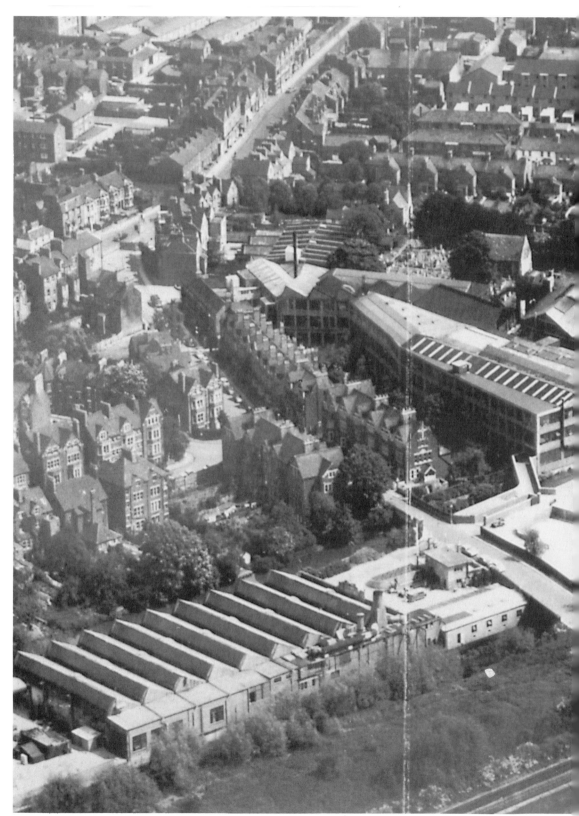

An aerial view of W. Lucy & Co. Ltd. taken about 1960.

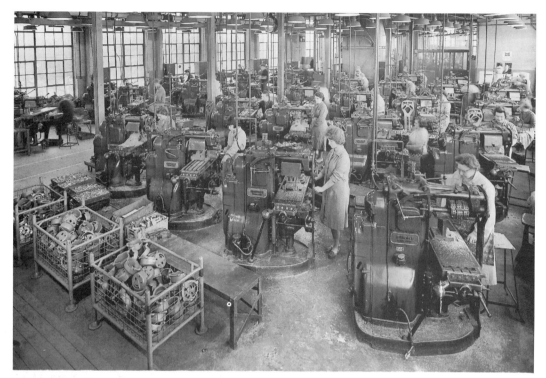

The Milling Department. The two ladies at the front right are S. Dean and Glad Bartlett.

Switchgear Assembly, early 1960s. Working backwards on the left-hand side, left to right: ?, C. Trafford, D. Bourton, G. Cameron, C. Pledge, A. Smith, R. White. Working backwards on the right-hand side, left to right: G. Martin, A. Baker, ?, M. Howes (in white coat), W. Druce, ?, ?, A. Drewett.

F.J. Payne & Son Limited

In 1921 F.J. Payne purchased the lease of a workshop in Worcester Place from St John's College for £850, the premises having previously been used by a Mr Parker repairing cars sold at a shop in St Giles. Mr Payne had trained in Leicestershire and had been in business as a motor mechanic and engineer in Alfred Street from 1914. The firm stayed in Worcester Place until 1971 when it moved to Mill Street, Osney. Under J. Payne an additional business making aids for the disabled began, moving to Eynsham in 1975. The engineering side of the business moved to this site a little later.

Taken in 1935, this photograph shows the Upper Floor on the engineering workshop. Left to right: Alf Reed from Botley who joined the firm in 1914 and stayed all his life; Philip Rogers from Long Handborough; F.J. Payne; Billy Bayliss an apprentice who lived in Friar's Entry and died in World War 2; Stan Pickett who came from Sutton, near Eynsham. The working hours were approximately 8 to 5.30. The workshop became more and more cramped as the years passed which made working very difficult. The premises were reputedly haunted. In 1928 a new glass roof was fitted by a specialist contractor from London. One man stayed overnight and slept in a car in the workshop. In the morning when the workers arrived they found this man outside and he insisted he had been chased out by a ghost. Some years later John Payne was working late and heard the stairs creak as someone came up them; when he went out there was no one there.

R.J. Johnson & Co.

Johnson's of Oxford is mentioned in a 1846 directory as a going concern. At this time the firm dealt in timber, slate and coal; different premises were occupied before the move to Worcester Place and the subsequent move to Cowley in 1965. Timber was the mainstay of the business and with the growth of building in North Oxford in the second half of the 19th century was much in demand. Agents from estates in the surrounding countryside came to order wood: 'A small cellar behind the office in the timber yard provided the wherewithal for their liquid refreshment, such visits being quite a social occasion and renewal of long standing associations'. Any timber ordered was delivered by horse-drawn wagon. The company had its own horses which were kept in the yard stables. Timber which originated in Russia and Northern Europe was taken by river even in the early years of this century until the railways became the means of transport: by World War 2 transport by road was more common. After the war the company began to diversify with more products, joinery, etc. By the 1960s the success of the business meant that Worcester Place was too cramped and new premises were required. In 1965 the business moved to Watlington Road, Cowley where the firm continues to enjoy success.

No. **4574**   OXFORD, *July 25th* 1893.

Mr Stanley

Please receive

FROM **R. J. JOHNSON & CO.,**

TIMBER AND SLATE MERCHANTS.

90 — 12 } ⁴⁄₄ x 1 *Wht Pine Bds*
30 — 19 }

12 *Bundling Lath*.

Per

A Johnson's invoice.

A group of employees outside the front of the Worcester Place premises. Left to right: ?, Stan Parkhurst, Ernie Bateman, Harry Hodges, Jack Greenwood (later yard foreman), Fred Boswell.

A Johnson's employee.

A.M. Kearsey & Son

Augustine Margot Kearsey was born in 1866 at Hailey. The 1891 census shows him lodging at 152 Walton Street and working as a groom. Shortly afterwards he married Eliza Russell at Witney and they had eight children born between 1892 and 1909. About 1898 Augustine Kearsey opened a furniture shop at 4 Albert Street, Jericho and a second shop in due course; the business was one of Oxford's oldest established furniture shops. Augustine Kearsey died in 1946 and the business continued in the family until about 1956.

Inquiries and Inspection Invited.
—
Quality and Satisfaction Guaranteed.
—
Iron Safes and Office Goods

Est. 1893

A. M. Kearsey & Son,
Furniture Dealers,
47 WALTON STREET,
Phone   OXFORD.   55784
———
Specialists in
Good Class Secondhand Furniture

The premises at 47 Walton Street.

Augustine Kearsey standing by the shafts of the cart.

Hinkins & Frewin Limited

Hinkins & Frewin was founded in 1849. In 1924 there was a need for additional accommodation and premises at the bottom of Cranham Street adjoining the Oxford—Birmingham Canal were acquired where a large woodworking plant and timber storage depot were erected. By 1929 still larger premises were required and the workshop in Cranham Street was doubled in size and modernised. Hinkins and Frewin have been involved with many important building works both in and around Oxford such as Banbury County School, the Society of Friend's School at Sibford Ferris and the Congregational Church at Cowley. By 1931 around 300 people were employed.

Above, a corner of the timber yard.

Looking towards Hinkins & Frewin in Canal Street.

A Hinkins & Frewin
advertisement.

A view of the
machine shop.

The softwood
joinery shop.

Stephenson's of Oxford

Stephenson's of Oxford was founded by William Stephenson who set up in business as a coal and builder's merchant in 1876. Although the company continued to trade under his name, no pictures survive of the founder and very little information too. By 1879 a yard was established at No. 30 Juxon Street and on 3rd December that year William Stephenson registered two narrow boats, *The Emerald* and *The Waterman* to carry coal and hardware on the Coventry, Oxford and Ashby Canals under the captaincy of Joseph Humphries, a well know boatmaster from Thrupp. An 1880 directory lists him as a coal and coke merchant trading from 17 Leckford Road, a few streets away. By 1882-83 the business had moved to Juxon Street and William Stephenson was additionally described as a wood, lime and brick merchant. Jericho by this time was expanding rapidly; the city's population quadrupled in the nineteenth century. Houses here and in Summertown, terraced and built fairly cheaply in red and yellow bricks, were springing up to provide homes for workers in such firms as the Oxford University Press. The relaxation of the rules forbidding fellows of Oxford Colleges to marry precipitated the development of North Oxford and the building of the large houses. William Stephenson was ideally placed to supply these areas with the goods they so vitally needed. No:30 Juxon Street where Stephenson lived was linked to the yard by a wall and office and he died here in 1900 aged 78. With no children to inherit, the business duly came under the control of John Wooldridge, a builder from Burford who had moved to Oxford in the 1880s. Despite the building side of the business being his main interest the sale of coke and coal were still very important to the firm and James Smith, who had worked for William Stephenson, managed this side of things.

In 1912 Stephenson's became known as Stephenson and Co. (Oxford) Limited being registered as a private company with a capital of £3,000 one pound shares. John Wooldridge held 1,000 shares until he died and remained the controlling director with James Smith as Company Secretary and manager at a salary of £104. per annum. By 1916 the firm's turnover was £11,000 and two horses and carts and six staff were employed; freelance boatmen had superseded the firm's own barges. After World War 1 a solid-tyred six ton vehicle was acquired from the Slough Trading Company and in due course more motor vehicles; despite this the horse and cart and pony and trolley continued in use. Stephenson's coal was carried by Fred Beauchamp of Thrupp, occasionally with assistance from his brother Joe. The longest journey they undertook was 110 miles. This took about a fortnight, earning them between £7 and £8! Four men were hired on a casual basis to unload the coal at the Juxon Street wharf and they received half a crown beer money to share when they started and 24s 6d when they finished. Fred Beauchamp spent the winter carrying building supplies for Stephenson's. Tiles came 30,000 to the boatload and sacks of cement, eleven to the ton, were winched by hand into the cement shed. In the journal of the Oxford Chamber of Commerce, 1932, the editor wrote 'I visited Juxon Street Wharf and was suprised at the quantity of the building material stored there. The manager told me that the stock on the wharf was the largest of its kind in Oxfordshire. The situation is unique, being alongside the Canal.' In 1938 the lease on Juxon Street was due to expire and new premises were therefore needed. Eventually these were found on Botley Road; the firm continued to expand celebrating its centenary in 1976. Sadly, within a decade, Stephenson's had ceased to exist.

E. Norridge, the first out-rider or sales representa-tive in the early 1920s. He joined the firm as office boy becoming managing director in 1934.

Staff loading a bath in 1928.

The Juxon Street Wharf in the 1920s.

Other Employment

The Oxford Co-operative Society at No.40—42 Walton Street taken around 1910. There were assembly rooms above the shop which could be rented out for weddings and parties. No. 37 Walton Street was reported to be haunted, with several members of the same family being aware of knocking and footsteps, as well as seeing a figure.

Brian Nutt ran a butcher's shop on the corner of Wellington Street and Albert Street in the mid-1960s when he sold it and it became Ali Stores. (Courtesy of the *Oxford Mail.*)

Situated next to St Sepulchre's Cemetery, North Oxford Grocery Fruit and Plant Stores Limited at No. 78 Walton Street in 1958. The little girl in the upstairs window is Angela McGuinness and the shop assistant is either Mrs Sheila McGuiness or Eileen Baker.

Bob Jones' cycle shop about 1976. As the notice suggests, cycles could be hired here but additionally the shop was also an ironmongers where wood and paraffin were sold.

Oxford University Press

Following the printing of the first book in Oxford in 1478, in 1586 the Star Chamber court granted Oxford University the privilege of printing books. Further charters were granted and in 1633 Delegates were appointed. In the late 17th century printing was carried out in the basement of the Sheldonian Theatre but within a couple of generations the Clarendon Building in Broad Street had been built and the printing transferred there. Named after the Earl of Clarendon whose successful publication *History of the Great Rebellion* provided some of the finance for the building, this was the home of the Oxford University Press (OUP) until 1830.

The OUP moved to Jericho when the premises in Walton Street were erected in the years 1827–32. Built in a collegiate style around a courtyard, the two divisions of the Press occupied different wings; the Bible Press the South Wing and the Learned or Classical Press the North Wing. During the first half of the 19th century, the OUP was run by partners who had shares in the business. These partners were all master printers and the most famous of them, especially in connection with Jericho, was Thomas Combe. Until the construction of the new Press building the only houses in Jericho consisted of Jericho House, the coal wharves along the canal and a few houses for canal workers; the rest of the area was agricultural. However, once the Press was constructed new housing began to appear and the rapid expansion of the same led Thomas Combe to give his support to the building of St. Barnabas Church.

Although initially there was no publishing side of the business this changed as educational reforms meant a great demand for school text books. This demand and the subsequent increase in business was so great that a division of the press was opened in London handled by Alexander Macmillan, an established publisher, and the OUP became a major publishing house. In 1977 the London office was transferred to Oxford.

'In 1873 The Clarendon Arms was built by Mr Parker, a former Partner, in order to supply the Press with good wholesome beer' as no alcohol was allowed on the premises; in 1963 The Clarendon Arms was converted into offices. During World War 1, 356 male employees served and 45 died; during World War 2 256 Press members served and 18 died. The War memorial at the Press was unveiled by Admiral Sir Reginald Hall on 5 October 1920; £122 10s had been subscribed by the members of the Press. The OUP recognised early on the need for academic books in other corners of the globe and offices were set up, gradually publishing academic books by local authors as well as helping with educational books for schools. Some of these offices can be found in the United States, Japan, Nigeria, Malaysia and India.

The original buildings have been considerably enlarged and altered since they were built. Expansion has seen the annual production of books increase from 250,000 books in 1918 to 1.5 million in 1948 and 4 million in 1958. The requirements of a modern day publishing house are of course totally different and computers have superseded the tools of trade so familiar to those of only a generation or so ago. The success of the OUP continues in such diverse subjects as dictionaries, medical and children's books, great classics, music and poetry.

An early view of the OUP buildings. (Courtesy of OUP Archives.)

This photograph was probably taken in the Orchard or North Yard around 1862. From left to right, back row: John Thomas, pressman (one of 4 brothers in the printing trade); Henry Crozier, compositor; Duncan Anderson, compositor; Abraham Parker, compositor and landlord of the Clarendon Arms; Hamilton Thomas Woods, compositor; Decimus Roberts, compositor. Front row: Joseph Goodger, porter at the Lodge; Francis Thomas, Learned Side warehouseman; John Cripps Pembrey, reader formerly a compositor. (*The Clarendonian*, 1960s.)

Press band 1874. Back row, left to right: J. Thomas; W. Sheppard; H. English; G.H. Akers; G. Brooks. Middle row: G. Denton; J. Miller; G. Marygold; T. Shurrock; A. Chidwick; G. Payton; G. Thomas; T.L. Aldridge; W.E. Walker; H.J. Denton. Front row: A. Shurrock; R. Draper; E. Pickard Hall; L. Denton. (Courtesy of OUP Archives.)

The Learned Side Warehouse Staff 1914. Back row, left to right: Fred Cox; David Walker (member of the Press Fire Brigade); Jack Price. Front row: Francis Wakelin; Albert Harris (Hon. Sec. of the Press Fire Brigade until 1915 when he obtained a commission in the Sherwood Foresters); Frank Phipps. (Courtesy of OUP Archives.)

OUP Woodstock Charity Cup Winners 1923. Left to right, back row: A.H. Harvey; C.F. Jacobs; A.W. Foster (Sec.); F. Poulter; H.F. Weller; G. Mattock; E.T. Nursen; R.A. Cleaver; G.A. Wicks (linesman). Front row: A. Panting; W. Neale; W.H. Masters; E.H. Fathers; C. Davis; J. Pimm; P. Cox. (Courtesy of OUP Archives.)

OUP Football Team 1929–30. Left to right, back row: W.T. Wilkins (Hon. Sec.); A.P. Janaway; L. Stevens; J. Day; A. Massey; D. Murphy; H. Battersby. Middle row: H. Harvey; G. Peach; C.S. Collet (Capt.); C.F. Collins; R. Rawlings. Front row: F.H. Sanson; E. Harvey. (Courtesy of OUP Archives.)

OUP Bowls Team 1922. Left to right, back row: H. Weller; L. Perry; J. Thomas; H. Simms; E. Goddard; H. Taylor; H. Curtis; J. Hawtin; A. Cleaver. Front row: A. Lusty; J. Money; A.H. Harvey; W. Walker; E. Money. (Courtesy of OUP Archives.)

The Home Guard, July 1940, was attached to the West Company of the Oxford Battalion. They performed nightly guard duties at the Press throughout the war. The group includes G.P. Keep, H. Simms, A. Deacon, E. Harris, T. Wells, T. Bennett, W.G. Colett, R. Molt, F. Margetts, W. Simms, W. Hearn, W. Colmer, S. Best, B.H Gray and F. Carter. (*The Clarendonian,* 1960s.)

Machine Room Outing 30th June 1928. From left to right, front row: F. Heath; G. Peach; G. Soden; H. Sparkes and D. Eadiss. Second row: W. Laith; W. Buckingham; J. Hedges; L. Taylor; G. Thomas; J. Borthwick; T. Chandler; E. Rogers; F. Allen; H. White. Third row: W. Roper; H. Battersby; W. Goddard; J. McGregor; W. Cleaver; J. Horwood; E. Hallett; W.T. Hine; C. Foster; G. Hine; J. Thomas; F. Thomas; W. Ward; S. Goddard; R. Surman; F. Dunning; H. Weller. Back row: F. Clifford; H. Barson; F.P. Clifford; J. Edmunds; F. Jacob; V. Clements; A. Rivers; F. Candsell; A. Bolton; G. Hope; F. Cooke; W. Town; J. Vaughan and R. Marshall. (*The Clarendonian,* 1960s)

The Wayzgoose and the Pomegranate pantomime performed at the 1963 children's Christmas Party. Left to right, standing: Philip Morton; Alan Jones; Ron Smith; Mark Foster; Tony Bennell; Fred Lee; Terry Foster. Kneeling: Ray Church; Philip Porter; Garvin Reeves; Tony Hopcroft; Jeff Wharehall. Front: Jerry Fulton. (*The Clarendonian,* 1960s.)

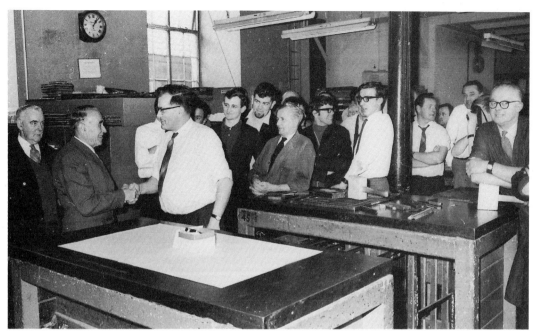

The retirement of Jack Powell in the mid-1960s in the mono-annexe. Left to right: Len Griffin; Jack Powell; Phil Walker (father of the Chapel); Robert Boyd; Roger King; Bill Morse; Tony Bennell; Wilf Langer; Alf Pill; Tony Wharton; Peter Brooker and Les Brogden. (*The Clarendonian,* 1960s.)

OUP engineers in the engineering yard between about 1920 and 1930. Standing second from the right is Lionel Green who worked at the OUP for 40 years. Seated second from the right is Lionel's father, Joe Green, who was employed by the OUP for between 70 and 80 years!

Women employees in the bindery, late 1920s or early 1930s. (Courtesy of OUP Archives.)

Inside a machine room around the turn of the century, note the penny farthing! (Courtesy of OUP Archives.)

The first Flower show was held in the quad on 7 September 1918; the last was held on 31 August 1929. (Courtesy of OUP Archives.)

In October 1885 the OUP Fire Brigade received official status. The first fire engine was provided by the Delegates for use at the Press in 1830. (Courtesy of OUP Archives.)

Oxford University Press St. John's Ambulance 1957. Top row: third from right Richard Carr; ?; Ernie Spiers. Front row: second from left Arthur Young. The Press Division started in 1908.

Fire Brigade competition about 1971 with Steve Carr from Oxford University Press.

Religion and Education

The Old Jewish Synagogue. (Photograph by Ivor Fields.)

There has been a synagogue in Jericho since around 1883 when an upstairs room on the west side of Worcester Place, possibly owned by a Mr Parker, was used. Almost ten years later No. 1 Nelson Street was leased for 5 years at £28 per annum plus rates. This building was built in 1891 by a local builder, John Job Gardner on a piece of land originally part of the Great Bear Meadow. Although not purpose built, an application for building permission in 1891 describing it as a Proposed Mission Room, it served the Jewish community for nearly 80 years. Plans were begun in the early 1960s to acquire land adjacent to the synagogue. In May 1966 No. 3 Nelson Street and builder's yard was bought but it was not until the death of an elderly widow three years later that further property could be purchased which enabled the new plans to be put in motion. The demolition of the old building started at the end of 1971.

St. Barnabas Church

The building of the Clarendon Press between 1827 and 1832 stimulated the building of housing so that it soon became apparent that a church was required to serve the fledgling community's spiritual needs. The first church built in Jericho, St Paul's in Walton Street, was consecrated in 1836. As the population continued to expand, it became obvious that another church was needed.

The building of St. Barnabas was largely due to the efforts of Thomas Combe, the Superintendent of the Clarendon Press. He was very interested in the views of J. Newman and Dr Pusey who had shared lodgings with him in Oriel Street and it was through his interest in the Oxford Movement that he planned that the new church would use the ceremonials they favoured. William Ward gave a plot of land in Cardigan Street and Arthur Blomfield was employed as the architect. There was a deliberate plan to keep the exterior as plain as possible, reserving all the grandeur for the interior; St Barnabas was built in an early form of church architecture called the Basilica and accommodated 1,000 persons. The church cost £6,492 7s 8d and the 132 feet campanile, added three years later, £788 18s 7d. The church was first painted by members of the Engineering staff of the OUP. Thomas Hardy used St Barnabas in Jude the Obscure calling it St Silas and describing it as 'the church of ceremonies'.

The church's foundation stone was laid in April 1868 and eighteen months later St Barnabas was consecrated. At this ceremony the sexes were segregated with the females on the northern side and the males on the southern side. Prior to this the clergy had walked from St Paul's in an imposing procession with banners and a cross whilst singing Onward Christian Soldiers. There was some opposition to the leanings of the church and cartoons such as 'Barnabas Junction. Change here for Rome' and another depicting a spider's web spun between St Barnabas and St Peter's, Rome showed the traditional fear of anything 'Popish' that many English people still retained.

St George's Chapel was added in 1919, commemorating the church's first 50 years and as a memorial to those parishioners who had been killed in World War 1.

The first vicar was Father Montague Henry Noel who remained at St Barnabas for thirty years. He made a deep impression on the whole parish and was remembered with affection by the older residents many decades later. The children's services on Sunday afternoon were extremely popular and the church was well loved by them; they referred to it as 'Our Barnabas'.

In 1964 the parishes of St Paul and St Barnabas were united, the latter becoming the church of the parish. St Paul's was returned to the Radcliffe Infirmary who had originally given the site and was subsequently developed.

From the beginning the church attracted people from outside the parish as well as parishoners with residents of North Oxford arriving in their carriages and undergraduates.

St Barnabas Church on St Barnabas' Day 1907 looking along Canal Street.

Looking at St Barnabas from the canal about 1869.

The interior of St Barnabas probably taken in the latter part of the nineteenth century. Looking east towards the altar which is raised nine steps above the nave, the open metal-work cross suspended from the roof of the church can be seen.

The lying in state of Thomas Combe who died 29 October 1872; he left £80,000 in his will.

Thomas Combe.

Thomas Combe was buried in St Sepulchre's cemetery which was opened in the 1840s when most of the city churchyards were full to overflowing. Many famous names are buried here, including Benjamin Jowett, Master of Balliol. The ancient manor of Walton lay to the north of Jericho and until the eighteenth century was entirely farm land. The principal farmhouse and buildings stood near where the cemetery is now.

The first five vicars of St Barnabas taken about 1919. Back row, left to right: Rev. H.C. Frith (1911–1916), Rev. A.G. Bisdee (1917–1946). Front row: Rev. C.H. Bickerton Hudson (1899–1901), Rev. Montague H. Noel (1869–1899), Ven Archbishop C. Hallett (1902–1911).

Father Noel was particularly well loved. After the children's services on Sunday afternoon he would go to Port Meadow to play football with the boys. He was also a dab hand at pulling teeth. 'In his middle life Father Noel developed a hobby for tooth extracting. He procured a set or two of forceps and for a good many years was the principal dentist for the parish, not only for boys and young girls, but for many adults also. Many who feared a dentist would not object to having a tooth out unofficially. It was wonderful too what luck he had. Almost invariably the extraction was a successful one and I never heard of any complication arising afterwards.'

St Barnabas School History

'Second only in importance to the Church itself are the Schools of St Barnabas'. A school had been built for St Paul's in the 1850s due to the generosity of Rev. Venables, later the Bishop of Nassau, and was later transferred to St Barnabas parish. Father Noel himself donated about £700 towards the building of a new St Paul's School. More land was given by Rev. Venables and a girls' and infants' school was built; the girls' and boys' schools were amalgamated in 1928.

The first log book, kept by the Headmaster William Wheatley, dates from 1873 and records the conditions and illnesses affecting the pupils. In January 1873 there were 124 boys (no numbers are available for the girls or infants); by 1900 there were 211 boys, 248 girls and 259 infants, totalling 718 children in a school which was considered overcrowded in the mid-1870s with 168 children in virtually the same amount of space. In 1928 the school was divided into a mixed upper and lower school; numbers fell but during World War 2 evacuees helped to swell the numbers. In 1962 children over 11 were transferred to a secondary school in the city and St Barnabas became a primary school.

St Barnabas was, and still remains though to a lesser extent, a church school and it is clear from the school log books that the relationship between church and school was very close. The St Barnabas clergy taught in the school and either the vicar or one of his curates took morning prayers each day. The children attended church for the various religious festivals and on Good Friday 1874 all the children attended twice; school life was closely connected with the church calendar. Nowadays this attendance is reduced to twice termly. Although the vast majority of pupils were the children of the labouring class, the education offered by St Barnabas was suprisingly good. The curriculum was also varied; in July 1873 a Drum and Fife Band was formed which played at the various church festivals; by 1878 music was very important with constant singing lessons and practices. In 1884 science was introduced followed by French and Latin a year later. Former pupils remained involved with the school, one arranging a visit to the Bodleian, another who owned a cycle shop provided 12 bicycles in 1920 for the boys to ride to Abingdon and in 1926 one organised a visit to the University Museum.

Extracts from Boys' School Log Book.

March 14th 1873. One case of insubordination has occurred this week by a boy refusing at first to hold out his hand for punishment but after a good talking to and a few a stripes he speedily came round.

December 6 1876. The results of the examinations are far from satisfactory.

There was not always good attendance and the head had to send round for absentees. One boy 'suffers from his head and is subject to night terrors, going over his lessons in his sleep. The mother asked to excuse him some of the work'.

'Mr Harris informed me that his son George has inflammation of the lungs and is not expected to live.'

Extracts from the Girl's School Log Book.

1900. Miserable weather, rain and sleet constantly falling resulted in the presence of a very small number of children, 47 being present.

7th January 1901. School reopened. Just as the children should have been coming to school the snow was falling heavily and only 155 children were present.

St Barnabas Infants' School, October 27th 1924. Back row, second from right Doreen Harris; the girl on the horse is Joan Shorter. Fourth on the left at the front is Doris Hanks and on the far left Phyllis Hanks. Second on the left in the middle row is Vera Eaglestone. The teacher on the left is Miss Packer.

St Barnabas Girls School, Class IV 1927. Left to right, front row: Phyllis Jones, ?, Phyllis Carr, ?, ?. Second row: Phyllis Hanks, ?, ?, ?, Rita Eaglestone, ?, ?, Winnie Saunders. Third row: ?, ?, ?, ?, ?, ?, – Alder, ?, Betty Seaward. Back row: ?, ?. Alma Hunt, ?, Betty Howes, ?, Christine Hann. The teacher is Miss Cripps.

St Barnabas School, late 1940s. Fourth from the left in the front row is Deanna Clarke. The teacher is Doreen Wyatt.

Geography lessons in the 1950s! Left to right: Isabel Smith, ?, Geoffrey Mercer, Dennis Shelton, ?, Jean Grisewood.

St Barnabas School, late 1950s. Left to right, back row: Stephen Carr, Susan Perks, Susan Hobson, ?, Anne Saunders, Hazel Truby, Chris Goodwin, Roger Saint, ?, Sylvia Amos. Middle row: Tina May?, John Smith, Angela Clarke?, ?, ?, Helen Brown, ?, Steve James, Billy Peddy, Chris Agutter. Front row: Michael Oliver, ?, William Bricknell, John Beal, Gerald Perks, Geoff Collins, Royce Henderson.

Music was a very important subject at St Barnabas. In this photograph of the Junior's Percussion Band taken in the mid-1950s are, left to right, first row: Pat Webster, Norma Paddon, ?, Sheila Riley, Janet Grimshaw, Marion Cornborough, Andrew Kingsman, Shirley Perks, Constance Ballard, Maureen Molyneux. Second row: Valerie Wright, ?, ?, Dennis Shelton, Jennifer Rush, Peter Preston, Jean Grisewood, Caroline Peddy. The teachers are Miss Brucker and Mr Foster.

This photograph of Class 4, again in the 1950s, includes Warren Palmer (seated front left), Paul Kingsman, Lucy Cooper, Geoff Cripps (third desk back on the right), and Valerie Wright. Standing, John Cadd, ?, John Rush, ?.

Christmas 1955. 'The Adoration of the Baby' with Mary Huckin as Mary, John Rush as Joseph, Anne Marie Knibbs as the Angel Gabriel. The King on the left is John Cadd and second from the right is 'Tossie'.

A similar scene in the late-1950s: Alan Wakefield as Joseph, Linda Jones as Mary, Angela Goodman as the Angel Gabriel. The angel to the bottom right is Marion Cornborough; angels from the left: ?, Susan Dean, Sylvia Smallbone, ?, Rita Daniels. Malcolm Surman is the third king from the right and kneeling front left is Pauline ?.

These religious tableaux were photographed in the Red Barn, the original Oxford Playhouse, situated behind St Giles' parish rooms. This popular event was held every two or three years, Father Bisdee having an interest in drama, and were performed for several evenings. Here the angels are bringing the word to the shepherds.

This photograph shows Christ's presentation at the temple. The child kneeling on the right is Betty Woodward. All the costumes were made by the parents.

St Barnabas Football Team 1955–56. Left to right, back row: Wallace, Luke, Cooke, Knibbs, Ryman, Dean. Front row: Hopes, Peedell, Preston (Captain), Jewell, Newell. The team played nine matches and won six of them.

St Barnabas Football Team 1956 Left to right, back row: Barry Jones, Thomas Hope, Richard Hathaway, ?, ?, Gerald Black. Front row: Alan Wakefield, Raymond Newell, Billy Preston, Tony Harris, Gordon Kitching.

St Barnabas Girls' Hockey Team photographed in the mid-1950s. Left to right, back row: Rosemarie Ballard, Carol Wright, Ann Smart, Janet Coates, Valerie Smith, Julie Bateman. Front row: Christine Rawlings, Helen Smith, ?, Anita Issacs, Wendy Shirley, Gillian Cornborough.

St Barnabas Church Football Team 1911–12. Hubert Charles Harris is on the right sitting in the front row. Also included here is the Rev. Michell.

Miss Brucker at the presentation to mark her retirement in 1959. From the right: Sheila Riley, Vi Court, − Wheeler, Diane Whitbread. Miss Brucker started her training as a Student Teacher at St Barnabas whilst still a pupil at Oxford High School for Girls. She returned to the school after college as a teacher of 53 five-year olds at a salary of £150. Although the buildings were very old the teaching methods were very modern and teachers and students from other schools often visited to see the reading and number activities.

Mr Huckin and Mrs Rush at the same event.

JERICHO GARDENS (Jericho), from 92 Cardigan street.

1 Clarke Edwin Albt. Wm
2 Newbold Frank
3 Allen Alfd
4 Castle William
5 Fletcher Thomas Edwd
6 Payne Ignatius
7 Pickett Mrs
8 Green Charles
9 Higgs Henry Edward
10 Bell James
11 Burgess Leonard
12 Knight Sam
..... here is Jericho st .....
13 Fawdrey Edgar
14 Wright Ernest
15 Bayliss William
16 Slatford Mrs. Daisy
17 Allen Joseph
18 Haydon Robert
19 Goswell Miss
20 Burgess William
21 Evans Mrs
22 Charles John Thomas
23 Mazey James
24 Baker Hy
..... here is Cardigan st. ....

JERICHO ST. (Jericho), from 55 Walton street.
.... here is King st ....
1A, Dunsby Albt
1 Collins Mrs
2 Dawson Mrs
3 Belcher Joseph
4 & 5 Cleaver W. E. I. garage
6 Sansom Charles
7 Page Charles
.... here is Jericho grdns ....
8 Fawdrey Danl
.... here is Union st ......
8A, Walters Arth
9 Huckin Frank
10 Mayo John
11 Dawson Thomas James
12 Simms Walter
13 Timms Albert E
14 Welford Benj.Jsph.John
15 Bricknell Mrs
16 Beale Frederick George
16 Cooper Jas.chimney swp
17 Harvey Mrs
18 Coles William
19 Ward Albert John
20 Woodley James Edward
21 Peedell Walter Edward
.... here is Albert st ....
22 Stowell Mark A
23 Strange Harry
24 Higgs George
26 Whiting Mrs
27 Clark Frederick
28 Davis Jesse
29 Drinkwater Percival
30 Templeton David
  Howkins Wm. decrtr. (workshop)
...... here is Cranham ter ......
32 Levens Wm. grocer
  Rawlins J. & Son, bldrs. (works)
32A Bradfield Edwd. Wm

33 Richards Mrs
34 Alford Miss
35 Sorrell Mrs
36 Attwood William
37 Bennett Mrs
38 Bowers William John

CANAL ST. (Jericho), from Nelson street.
1 Robinson Edward
1A, Halsey William
... here is Gt. Clarendon st ...
2 Hamilton William Henry
3 Foster Arthur
4 Cole Charles
5 Capel Richard
6 Saunders Mrs
7 Buckett Percy James
8 Whitman Mrs. R. A
9 Bowell Charles, beer ret
...... here is Cardigan st ......
...... here is Dawson pl ......
10 Keep William Samuel
11 Sanders Mrs
12 Hutt John
13 Parslow Hy. Wltr
14 Ward Jesse James
.... here is Ferry rd ....
15 Hann Wm. Jn
16 Wells Mrs
17 Burden Alfred
18 Morley Richard
19 Phipps Frank Arthur
  Hinkins & Frewin Ltd. builders. See advert
20 Billings J. E. & Co. Ltd. builders
.... here is Mount pl ......
21 Simmonds Harry, grngro
22 Tombs Francis
23 Hawkins Frederick
...... here is Cranham st ......
.... here is Victor st ....
25 Mobley Owen, shopkpr
26 Harrison Albert
27 Williams Thos. Geo
28 Miller Edwin Richard
29 Perks Miss
30 Mazey Fredk. W
31 Woodward Thomas
32 Taylor Albt. Fredk
33 East Geo. Wm
...... here is Cardigan st ......
33A, St. Barnabas Parish Institute (Frederick C. Panter, caretaker)
34 Mobley Mrs. F
35 Crowther William F. M
36 Robinson Wm
37 Best Miss A
38 Drewett Geo. Isaac
... here is Gt. Clarendon st ...
39 Smart Miss
40 Brogden Mrs. dressma

CARDIGAN ST. from 48 Walton street.
SOUTH SIDE.
1 Landon John
2 Long Thomas
3 Harbrow Mrs
4 Sleath William
5 Montgomery Alex. B. S
.... here is King st ....
6 Johnson Hy. T. greengro

7 Fletcher Mrs
8 Hill William Joseph
9 Smith Joseph George
10 Mullard Albt. Wm. sen
11 Richards Joseph Thos. beer retailer
12 Faulkner Geo. R. grngro
12 Faulkner&Son,cycle agts
13 Faulkner Fredk. Chas
14 Papel Frank John
15 Hutt John
16 Kettle Mrs
17 Townsend Mrs
18 Surman Jn. L. S. jun
19 Simmonds Fredk.James
20 Ensor Mrs
.... here is Union st ....
21 Mayell Albert
22 Neal Mrs
23 Castle John William
24 Walker Mrs
25 Brooks Miss
26 Parsons Walt. Hy
27 Bowles Mrs. L
28 Baker Bertie Richard
29 Harris Mrs
30 Lay Mrs
31 Taylor Mrs
32 Pitt Leo
33 Udell George Edward
34 Bishop Alfred
35 Shirley Wm. undertaker
.... here is Albert st ....
36 Wastie Clement
37 Simms George Vincent
38 Harper Mrs
39 Gooch Edward
40 Hawes Wm. Chas
41 Beal George
42 Rich Henry Thomas
  St. Barnabas School (infants)
43 Kitchen Bertie John
44 Aubrey Mrs. E. M
.... here is Canal st ....
47 Tayler Thos. Alfd
48 Harbrow Arthur William
49 Chown Harry
50 Hopkins Gilbt. Victor
... here is St. Barnabas st ...
NORTH SIDE.
ST. BARNABAS' CHURCH
.... here is Canal st ....
51 Afford Mrs. Sarah, beer retlr
52 Eaglestone Albert Chas
53 Harris Miss
54 Price Thomas Henry
55 Bludworth Mrs. Rose
56 Wilkinson Albert
57 Hodgkins Miss, shopkpr
58 Trinder Miss L. A
59 Draper Henry
60 Long Arthur
61 Spindler Frederick Geo
62 Shuter Richard Henry
63 Bayliss Joseph Henry
64 Robbins Mrs
65 Whipp Jn. Chas
66 Harding Charles
67 Burgess Arnold W
...... he

Extract from Kelly's Directory, 1931.

Recreation

Empire Day 1925 taken at St Barnabas Infant School. Britannia is Mrs Sawyer and her two escorts are Betty Howes on the left and Alma Hunt on the right.

In this photograph dating from the early 1900s, these Jericho children are celebrating May Day. May Wilkins is in the centre as May Queen. Second from the left is her sister Nell. It is not clear exactly where this photograph was taken but in may be in Worcester College grounds.

This photograph taken in the mid-1920s shows some of the children from St Barnabas school. Dancing was something the school excelled at and the children used to perform at various locations such as the Observatory, now Green College, and at Worcester College. Here the boys are dressed as gardeners with besom brooms and the girls are daffodils; the dresses were yellow pleated silk and were made by a local dressmaker although the parents had to pay for them. It was considered an honour to be chosen and the cost was not begrudged. Although the children are pictured wearing shoes and socks this was due to the inclement weather as they usually danced barefoot. Left to right, back row: Alma Hunt, ?, ?, Christine Hann, ?, ?, ?, Jean Jupp, Betty Howes. Front row: ?, ?, Alex ?, Doris Hanks, ?, ?, – Rose.

A group of Jericho men. Second from left George Henry Harris, second from right John Pimm.

A photograph of a men's club taken outside the Crown Inn opposite St Barnabas Church. Front row, left to right: William Henry Hamilton, known as Henry or Harry (born 1856), a builder and decorator and a churchwarden, ?, Mr Herbert who ran the ferry across the Oxford to Birmingham canal. The Jericho ferry was a short cut to the railway station, the school bathing place and Port Meadow; the fare was 1p for adults. The vicar, third from the left in the middle row, is Ven. Archdeacon C. Hallett. When Mr Hamilton gave up the Crown he lived on Canal Street, in one of the biggest houses in Jericho.

A group of Jericho Rover Scouts taken about 1920. Left to right, front row: ?, Albert Eaglestone, ?, Bill Clifford. Back row: — Foster, — Foster, ?, Fred Bolton, ?, Len Youngman, Percy Best, ?.

Taken within a few years of the above, this group of Jericho Scouts are pictured training on Port Meadow; they entered Junior County Cross County Championships. Left to right: Len Youngman, Len Cantwell, Jack Clifford, Percy Bets, — Foster.

Jericho Scouts 1939. Left to right, back row: Eric Clark, A. Saunders, G. Halsey. Middle row: Arthur Carr, C. Blackwell, J. Simpson. Front row: Gordon Carr, B. Harris, F. Busby.

Taken about 1960 these cubs with spears are, left to right, standing: Steve Carr, Geoff Collins?, Philip Huckin, Graham Woodall, ?, Steve Ward, Keith Fortescue. Front row: Stephen Huckin, David Janes.

Jericho Cubs about 1962. This group includes Steve Carr and David Janes.

Brownies. Left to right, back row: Betty Seaward, ?, Betty Howes, — Leach. Middle row: ?, Winnie Saunders, ?. Front row: ?, Christine Hann, Rita Eaglestone.

Cubs outside St Barnabas with Father Broomfield. The cub at the back looking over his friend's shoulder is Paul Church the son of Syd Church, chauffeur at the Oxford University Press.

St Barnabas Guides. Left to right, front row: Maureen Goodway, Deanna Clarke, Fay Brockall, Pam Godfrey, Janet Cooper, ?, Pauline Martin. Second row: ?, Susan Deane, ?, ?, ?, ?, ?. Third row: ?, Valerie Kitching, Susan Green, ?, Jean Holloway, ?, Jean Tostin, Valerie Holloway, Jennifer Dunstan.

In this Guides photograph left to right: Frances Buckell, ?, Valerie Kitching, Jennifer Dunstan, Jean Tustin, ?, ?, ?, Maureen Goodway, Maureen Molyneux, Deanna Clarke.

Coronation Party in 1937 in King Street looking towards Great Clarendon Street.
The building on the right belonged to Harry Johnson who had a shop and delivered
groceries in his cart; the horse was led through the house (after moving the kitchen
table) and stabled at the rear. Those who have been identified include, to the left of
the table, May Johnson, Mary Soden, ?, Bert Dawson, the Castle twins. The girl
looking over the twins is Peggy Clifford. To the right of the table: Ken Preston,

Frank Quartermain, John Beesley (boy with hat), Betty Boswell, Gerald Clark, Barbara Fletcher. Standing on the right: ?, Les Brain, Mrs Mitchell, Mrs Ward (in grass skirt), Edith Beesley, Mrs Johnson (behind man with cap). The chef worked at Pheasant's fish and chip shop and later went to St John's College and then became landlord of the Bookbinder's Arms. One well known character from King Street was Fag End Lil who, as her name suggests, picked up cigarette ends.

Oxford Children's Festival Cranham Street party in July 1951. Those who have been identified include Colin Harris in the arms of his grandmother at left-hand front. The second table, first on the left at the front Ronald Ashmall, fourth on the left George Daniels, third on the right David Taylor. The last boy at the back is Michael Chennells. Other children include Malcolm Surman, Terry Criswood, Brian Taylor, Jean Coates as well as the landlady of the Globe, Mrs Cox. The party was organised

by Mrs S. Gardiner, Mrs G. Palmer, Mrs G. Hardiman, Mrs L. Cox, Mrs D. Ashmall, Mrs Grieswood and Mrs B. Gaskins. Malcolm Surman was the son of the landlord and landlady of the Harcourt Arms, Jericho Street. He was one of the Grenadier Guardsmen who carried Sir Winston Churchill's coffin from St Paul's cathedral; he later returned to the Oxford City police force.

Taken in Jericho Street at the junction with King Street from behind the Scala cinema which was built in 1913. Left to right, front row: ? (American boy), Kevin Beesley, Robin Cooper, Clyde Morgan, Steve Cartwright. Back row: Roger Saint, – Shelton, – Beal (the son of Reg Beal who was Father of the Chapel at the OUP). Before 1913 the Scala was known as the North Oxford Kinema. In the 1920s there was a twenty minute singsong backed by a nine piece orchestra between films; in 1927 the cinema was out of bounds to undergraduates.

The Harcourt Arms Aunt Sally team 1953. Left to right: Arthur Kitching, Bob Hastings, Jack Peedell, Aubrey Tustin, ?, Horace Peedell.

The Globe public house outing about 1955. This was an annual event and the destination was Ascot races. Second from left Eileen Blackburn, ?, Mrs Druce ?, and behind her with large hat Margaret Bean. The men at the far back are Percy Bean and John Peedell.

A Lucy's outing probably dating from the late 1940s. Included in this photograph are Bill Mitchell and Reg —.

The children's fancy dress competition at the Coronation Street Party in Jericho Street in 1953. The children include: Brenda and John Jones, David and Robert Cox, Alan and Raymond Peedell, Colin and Jean Tustin, Valerie and Geoff Kitching, Susan Dean, Carol Wright, Zena Strange, Sheila Clark, Christine and Maureen

Molyneux. The adults include: Reg Surman, Aubrey Tustin, Den Beale, Joan and Arthur Kitching, Ron Powell, Jack and Wally Peedell and Vera Dean. Father Nicholson is on the right and is the only retired vicar still living.

Inside the Fountain Public House in the late-1950s at a presentation to mark the departure of the landlord Leonard Beesley and his wife Edith (their son John became landlord later). Left to right, back row: Mrs Curtis. Front row: Olive Tompkins, Mrs Surrage, Mrs Beesley, Mrs Preedy, Mrs Harris, Mrs Preedy (who had 16 children). Behind Mrs Harris is Mrs Lock.

The same occasion with a group of male regulars. Left to right, front row: Philip Arnatt, Bill Smith, Ray Timms, Harold Bellinger, Ted Murphy, Bomber Harris. Back row includes: Bill Surrage, Les Wilkins, Arthur Curtis, Leonard Beesley, Percy Ensor, Sid Hook, Peter Ruanne, Arthur Beesley.

The front bar of the Fountain with Mr Bishop.

St Barnabas Gala Day in 1954. Jean Tustin is the Gala Queen and the Maids of Honour are Valerie Smith and Jennifer Dunstan.

St Barnabas Gala Day 1955; the children are watching a juggler. The photograph was taken in St Barnabas Senior School playground.

Aubrey and Kathleen Tustin as Pearly King and Queen at a late-1950s St Barnabas Gala Day.

Parents in fancy dress at the Gala Day in 1960. The photograph was taken at the rear of St Barnabas church; Aubrey Tustin is in the centre.

School children in fancy dress.

Steve Carr in fancy dress for the school fete in the 1950s, taken at the back of 27 Great Clarendon Street.

The Jericho Rejects, an amateur dramatic group, taken by Dennis Kennedy in 1995 whilst doing a play about VE day. (Courtesy of the *Oxford Mail.*) Left to right, bottom row: Wendy Gray, Sue Peed, Barry England, Eve Harris, Gwen Hill. Top row: Wendy Matthews, Jackie Eley, Sophie England, Chris Wheatley, Jean —, Jenny Guard, Barbara Dean.

A canal trip for Jericho residents to celebrate the Queen's Silver Jubilee in 1977 was followed by tea at St Barnabas School. (Courtesy of the *Oxford Mail.*) At the centre front Ted Harris and his mother Ethel Harris. The lady in the check coat is Mrs Smallbone, the lady on the far right by the narrowboat is Mrs Carter, second from the right Mrs Wilmer, third from the right Mrs Gladys Couling and behind her the vicar of St Barnabas, Father Michael Wright whose predecessor Father Hunt is at the back.

Jericho Life and Families

Some of the characters in Jericho have been the greengrocer from Canal Street 'Rhubarb' Simmons and his daughter 'Ningy'; 'Brassy' Toms; Jack 'Badger' Wall in Combe Road; Mr and Mrs Carter (she wore a man's cap) and their dog 'Wangy'. The rag and bone man came round and gave the children a windmill for jam jars. In Cardigan Street 'Fishy' Faulkner had a cycle shop and sold fruit and vegetables from a hand cart which had rabbits hung on the handles. The rabbits cost one shilling each or eleven pence if Mr Faulkner kept the skin. Mrs Hewitt's paper shop in Walton Street sold snuff which the apprentices and printers at the Oxford University Press bought as they were not allowed to smoke. They took snuff to counteract lead poisoning and as most of them were not so lucky as to own a snuff box, they poured the snuff straight into their waistcoat pocket. 'Old Timmy' wore a straw hat and sold kippers from a basket, or watercress when kippers were not available. A fat lady with a beard sold bananas from a hand cart. An Italian with a moustache parked by 15 Canal Street and played his barrel organ. A water cart like a tank came around and sprayed water on the streets to clean them. The women always swept the front steps every morning and would then scrub the step and brasso the handle. In the evening the women would put a chair on the path by the door and have a glass of beer and some bread and cheese.

Syd Church, chauffeur at the Oxford University Press.

From the earliest days of settlement in the area, flooding in Jericho, especially in the streets nearest the canal, was a problem. This photograph was taken in June 1955 in Cardigan Street and shows children returning from school. There are many references to flooding in reports in the 1870s and the 'poor or non-existent drainage and unsatisfactory water contributed to the illnesses that ran rife through the cramped and over-occupied housing'. In 1873 five of the eleven deaths from typhoid were from Jericho and in 1876 the area topped the table for deaths from infectious diseases. By 1877 all Oxford had been drained and for the first time there were no deaths from typhoid or diarrhoea in Jericho.

Large pipes were put into the streets in Jericho to combat the flooding. Here they are being put into Combe Road, one of the nearest streets to the canal, to successfully solve the problem.

These evacuees from London about 1942 were George and Emma Williamson who lived in Wellington Street. After the war they remained in Oxford.

The Carr family in the early 1940s. At the back is Tony Carr. Left to right Arthur, Phyllis, Michael and Gordon; the baby at the front is Iris. All the brothers except for Arthur worked at the OUP.

Taken in 1976, this photograph (courtesy of the *Oxford Mail*) celebrates the diamond wedding anniversary of Ferris Carr aged 80 and his wife Clara aged 81. The couple had lived in the same house, No. 76 Great Clarendon Street for the sixty years of their married life. Mr Carr was born in Wellington Street and worked as a warehouseman at the OUP for over 50 years.

Taken about 1950, the photograph shows, left to right, Doris Bridgewater and Michael Carr with canine friend. Rose Carr is half hidden on the left. St Barnabas school in the background.

Taken in the early 1950s, Iris Carr stands outside the New Inn with Nelson Street to the right.

The original houses in Nelson Street 'were largely built of materials obtained from houses that formerly occupied the site of the Martyr's Memorial'. Also in Nelson Street was the Parochial Hall presented to the parish in 1913 by an anonymous benefactor. Built by a Scottish evangelist Rev Henry Bazely in the 1880s it was known locally as the 'Burning Bush' because of a carving over the door. After his death it was used as a Meeting House by the Society of Friends, standing vacant for some years.

St Barnabas OAP Party. (Courtesy of the *Oxford Mail.*) Left to right: Gladys Couling, ?, Mrs Boswell, Councillor Fagg, Annie Harris, ?, ? (worked at the Cadena).

Fire in the OUP annexe, the Old Slaughter House in Walton Street, 19 February 1966. (Courtesy of the *Oxford Mail.*) The fire broke out in the positive store of the litho department. The press fire brigade was on the scene and had the water through by the time the City Brigade arrived. There was praise for the volunteers and the damage was not serious. For many years sheep from Gloucester Green were driven here for slaughter.

The Eaglestone family at 40 Cardigan Street. Left to right, front row: Albert Charles (1884–1962), Rose, Elizabeth, Joseph (a stonemason from North Oxfordshire), Essie, Fred. Back row: Florey, Reg and Maud.

The marriage of Maud Eaglestone and Frederick Spindler 30 August 1919. They courted for 18 years until he got a job with a wage they could live on. Left to right, back row: Eddie Hanks, ?, ?, ?, ?, ?, ?. Second row: ?, Doris Hanks, Essie Hanks (née Eaglestone), ?, ?, ?, ?, ?, ?, ?. Third row: Rose Wareham (née Eaglestone), ?, ?, Frederick Spindler, Maud Eaglestone, Elizabeth Eaglestone, Reg Eaglestone, Susan Alice Annie Eaglestone (née Hamilton) 1882–1965, Albert Charles Eaglestone 1884–1962. Front row: ?, Vera Eaglestone, ?, John Wareham, Albert Henry Eaglestone.

Pictured at 5 Allam Street, left to right: Doreen Harris, Annie Harris (née Pimm), Hubert Charles Harris and Hubert George Harris. H.C. Harris worked at the Oxford University Press.

Hubert Charles and Annie Harris in Juxon Street.

HARRIS, H. C. (L.S. Composing Room). Enlisted in the 4th Oxf. & Bucks L.I. on 31 Aug. 1914, and served in the 1/4th Bn. throughout : in England to 26 June 1915 ; in France to 20 Nov. 1917 ; and in Italy to 22 Feb. 1919. Engagements : Somme, 1916 ; Third Battle of Ypres, 1917 ; Austrian offensive, 1918. Appointed Lance-Corpl. ; Military Medal (for work on 10 Sept. 1918). Wounded, slightly, at Pozières, July 1916. Demobilized on 3 Mar. 1919. Resumed work at the Press.

War record of Hubert Charles Harris. (*The Clarendonian,* 1960s.)

The Hann family. Left to right, back row: George Hann, Dick French's father, Beatrice French, ?, Gladys Couling, Fred Hann. Front row: Mabel Hann, William Hann, Winnie Hann, Richard French, ?, ?, David Hann, ?.

William Hann, a chauffeur, moved to Jericho with his family from Sherborne in Dorset around 1912 when his employers moved to Oxford. In 1930 Gladys Hann married Harold Couling a shoemaker who did work for Lillingstones, a high class shoe shop. He started his own business at 15 Canal Street and eventually had a shop at the bottom of Richmond Road. Gladys is currently one of Jericho's oldest residents.

When Gladys was first married they lived in a room in Cranham Street. This photograph shows Gladys and her son Peter with 'Granny' Pearce the landlady.

A crowd outside St Barnabas Church in April 1954. On the left is the best man Ivan Roberts and on the right the bridegroom Thomas Blackburn, The Parochial Institute can be seen on the corner of Cardigan Street and Canal Street. This building dates from 1891 and was paid for by the Misses Greswell, the daughters of the Rev Richard Greswell; they also provided an endowment. Some of this money was used to purchase a house and the rent formed part of the Institute's income. The ground floor had a reading room and billiard room and was used as a men's club. The rest of the building was used as lodgings for one of the clergy and provided rooms for the caretaker. It was

also used for choir practices and meetings. By 1980 the building was in a very bad condition and some parishioners wished to sell it. It was, however, leased to the City Council, repaired and licensed back to the parish as a community centre.

Mr and Mrs Thomas Blackburn in Cardigan Street in the 1950s. The new St Barnabas school was built on this site.

In 1986 'The Dead of Jericho', an Inspector Morse story was filmed in Jericho. The top photograph is looking up Combe Road towards the Bookbinders Arms with John Thaw (Inspector Morse) and Kevin Whately (Sergeant Lewis).

This photograph looks down Combe Road towards the canal. In the book the murder took place in this road which was called Canal Reach. This was the first episode of the popular detective series and was broadcast on 6 January, 1987.